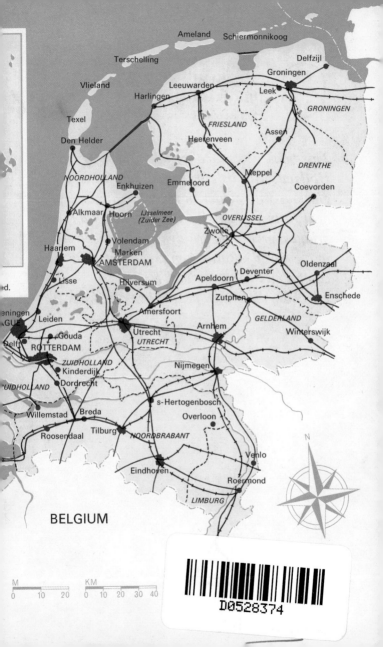

A Ladybird
'Easy-Reading' Book
Series 606G

*This book gives a colourful glimpse of
Holland, with its old towns, bulb fields
glorious with colour in the springtime,
neat farms, windmills, wide canals, many
bridges, great modern dykes, the greatest port
in the world – Rotterdam and a beautiful
capital city – Amsterdam. It also
tells how the Dutch people live and work.*

A LADYBIRD 'EASY-READING' BOOK

come to *HOLLAND*

by BETTY SCOTT DANIELL

with illustrations by JOHN BERRY

Publishers: Ladybird Books Ltd . Loughborough
© Ladybird Books Ltd (formerly Wills & Hepworth Ltd) 1971
Printed in England

COME TO HOLLAND

If you looked at Holland from an aeroplane, the first thing you would notice is that it is a very flat country. It would seem to be a patchwork of square fields and long, straight roads, and with canals everywhere. If you look at the map in the front of this book, you will see there is also a string of islands along the coast.

Holland, or the Netherlands as it is also called, is not a very large country. It is not very much larger than Wales. However, the population is very much greater—over 12 million people.

Although the countryside is flat, it is still full of interest and beauty. There are lovely, old towns, bulb fields glorious with colour in the springtime, neat farms, windmills, wide canals, many bridges, great modern dykes, the greatest port in the world—Rotterdam and a beautiful capital city—Amsterdam.

0 7214 0297 6

Almost half of Holland is below sea-level. Because of this, life for the Dutch people has always been a struggle against the invading sea.

Two thousand years ago, when the Romans came to this part of Europe, they found the native peoples living on man-made hills so that they and their homes would be safe from the water. Some man-made hills still remain. One is shown in the picture opposite. After a while, these people began to link together their man-made hills with roads or 'causeways' made of clay and stones. They found that by doing this they could keep the sea out of a much larger area of land.

These hills and causeways became the first 'dykes'. The land won from the sea and used for growing food and grazing cattle later became the first 'polders'. A polder is a low-lying area encircled by a dyke and from which the water has been pumped out. A great part of Holland consists of polders.

In olden days, during great storms and high tides, the earlier dykes used to break down and the land became flooded. Today, engineers are able to make strong dykes which can resist the heaviest battering from the sea.

In recent years many of these dykes (like the one in the picture) have been built, and there are now more than 1,500 miles of them. This means that more and more valuable land is being reclaimed.

There are now nearly 3,000 polders in Holland. Some cover only a few acres. Others are as large as 100,000 acres. Some even have new towns built on them.

Once the water has been pumped out, the soil is cultivated and becomes good farmland.

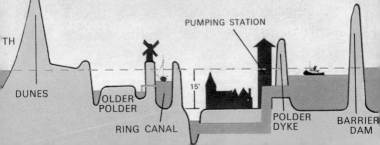

TH

PUMPING STATION

DUNES

OLDER
POLDER

RING CANAL

15'

POLDER
DYKE

BARRIER
DAM

In their fight against the sea, the Dutch have built dams as well as dykes. A dyke is a protective embankment around a polder or along the coast. A dam is a barrier across a river or a sea inlet.

If you looked at a map of the Holland of a hundred years ago, you would see a huge stretch of salt water right in the middle of the country. This was the Zuider Zee.

Now look at a modern map and you will see that this 'sea' has gone. Instead there is a lake called the IJsselmeer. A great dam was built to cut off the Zuider Zee from the North Sea. Then the salt water was pumped out. This has left only a lake, and where the rest of the water used to be is now good farmland.

Other big dams are being built in the south of Holland. Islands are being linked together to keep out the sea and reclaim more land. The dam in the picture is 18 miles long.

As a result of all this hard work, Holland is now an important farming country. Almost half the people who live there work on the land.

Many of the farms are new, because they are situated on recently-built polders. Most of this land is still below sea-level, so water must constantly be pumped out into ditches and away to the sea. In the old days this pumping was done by windmills, but nowadays it is done by powerful electric or diesel engines.

However, you can still see the old-fashioned windmills at work in some parts of Holland. The best place is at Kinderdijk, which is quite near Rotterdam. In some areas, windmills are also still used for grinding flour and sawing wood.

The rich soil in the polders grows good grass on which feed the famous Dutch Friesian cattle.

These black and white Friesian cows are good milk producers and from their milk is made the butter and cheese which Holland exports to many parts of the world.

You can see Dutch butter and cheeses on sale in our grocery shops and supermarkets.

Some Dutch cheeses look like big red footballs, and are made at a place called Edam, after which the cheese is named.

In the north of Holland is another place called Alkmaar, where there has been a famous cheese market for three hundred years. Our picture shows a market-day scene, with some cheeses being weighed.

The cheeses are piled on coloured wooden 'sledges' which have handles at each end. The sledges are carried by men wearing traditional costume and coloured hats. The men hook straps onto the handles of the heavy sledges, so that they can take the weight on their shoulders.

The Dutch like cheese so much that they often have it for breakfast.

The land reclaimed from the sea also provides the Dutch farmers with fields in which they can grow tulip and hyacinth bulbs.

The tulip fields in bloom are a wonderful sight. Thousands of visitors go to Holland each spring just to see the vast areas of red, yellow and pink blossoms. The flowers, as well as three thousand million bulbs, are exported to other countries.

Millions of carnations, chrysanthemums and sweet peas, gladioli and dahlias, are also exported.

Dutch market gardeners also grow fruit and vegetables for export as well as for sale in Dutch markets. They use large greenhouses, some of them covering as much as an acre of land each.

Some farmers use greenhouses built on tracks like railway lines. When a crop has been harvested, the greenhouses are wheeled over to shelter a newly-planted crop.

Holland is called the flower garden of Europe. Everywhere there are flowers, not only in the commercial flower fields but also in parks, public gardens and in the streets of the towns and cities too.

In every town and village there is a flower market, a mass of colour in spring, summer and autumn.

The best place in Holland to see flowers is a park called Keukenhof, at a place called Lisse. Keukenhof is a true flower park and is sometimes called the world's biggest flower-show. In it are millions of tulips, hyacinths and many other bulbs laid out in ornamental beds, some of them under trees or against a background of shrubs.

In one greenhouse at Keukenhof there are seven hundred different kinds of tulip. In these gardens, demonstrations of flower arranging are given by experts.

In their hard fight against the sea, the Dutch have not only won land from the water. They have also used the water to provide a wonderful system of canals for transport.

Not only the big cities like Amsterdam and Rotterdam have canals. The interior of the country still has many lakes, and these have been joined to one another by a dense network of inland waterways. Long before there were roads or railways, it was easy to travel by boat to any part of the Netherlands.

When one thinks of all these canals and lakes, and of the many long beaches on the North Sea coast, it is not surprising that swimming and boating are among the most popular sports in Holland.

Another popular pastime in Holland is skating.

In winter, when the many canals and lakes, and sometimes even the rivers, are frozen over, a great many people skate. School-children have one or two extra half-day holidays during the coldest weeks, so that they can enjoy this national sport. They always take a few small coins to give to the 'baanveger' (ice-sweeper), who keeps the tracks clear of the powdery ice caused by so much skating.

The greatest ice-skating event is the Eleven Towns Race held in Friesland. This covers a distance of 120 miles, starting and finishing at Leeuwarden.

Amsterdam is the lovely capital city of Holland.

Its many peaceful canals are crossed by four hundred bridges and lined with trees and graceful, old, red-brick buildings. In the 17th century these were the homes of wealthy merchants. Top floors were used for storing the tea, spices, silks and furs that the merchants' ships brought from the East. Because of the network of canals in Amsterdam, the ships were able to move along them right into the centre of the city.

Amsterdam still imports these goods and is still a famous centre for the cutting and polishing of diamonds. The diamond companies allow visitors to watch their skilled men cutting and polishing diamonds.

In summer the canals are cool and shady. People sit outdoors, in pavement cafés, enjoying huge cream cakes and ice-creams, or drinking coffee—which the Dutch love. They pay for anything they buy with *guilders* and *cents*.

A good way to get to know Amsterdam is to take a ride in one of the glass-roofed, sight-seeing boats. These pick their way through the maze of canals. Everywhere there seems to be something interesting and unusual to see.

Afterwards one should walk round Amsterdam to see more closely such sights as the Royal Palace with its colourful guards, the Tower of Tears from which Hendrik Hudson set sail in 1609 to discover the river that bears his name (on which New York now stands), the house of the painter Rembrandt and some of the most interesting museums in the world.

The Dutch port of Rotterdam is the greatest seaport in the world. Every year it receives about 30,000 ocean-going ships and 225,000 river and canal vessels.

The old port was destroyed by bombing in the Second World War. The new port has been planned to deal with 'container' traffic. This means that goods to be transported arrive ready-packed in huge, square, box-like containers which can be loaded and unloaded quickly and easily. A ship does not then have to spend so much time in port being loaded and unloaded.

Container-packed goods come to Rotterdam from countries in Europe, ready for loading onto ships going to countries overseas. Containers are also brought in the ships from countries overseas and unloaded at Rotterdam. They are then put on canal barges, river boats, railway wagons and lorries for transport to countries in Europe.

The old city centre of Rotterdam was also almost totally destroyed by bombs in World War II. In its place has been built a handsome, carefully planned city.

There are wide, main roads and large, open squares. Modern shopping areas, like the one in the picture, have been built for the convenience of pedestrians. All cars are banned from these centres.

In Rotterdam there is a famous high tower, called the Euromast, which is nearly 400 ft. high. From the top floor there is a breath-taking view of the harbours, the city and the countryside for miles around. The tower was built in only 23 days, 1 hour and 59 minutes! Nearby, the new University of Medicine was built in just one day longer!

In the past it was not possible to build many tall and very heavy buildings because the soil is so wet and marshy. The foundations would have sunk in the wet soil. Because there are still not very many tall blocks of offices and flats, the cities and towns spread wide across the countryside. In ten years the whole of the coastal area from Rotterdam as far north as Amsterdam will probably be one long city.

Not far from Rotterdam is The Hague. Here are the Dutch Houses of Parliament and the many government ministries. Here, also, the Queen of the Netherlands has a palace and receives ambassadors from other countries.

At The Hague there is a famous and most unusual town—Madurodam—the smallest town in the world! It is an exact model of a real town, everything in it being one twenty-fifth of its natural size.

Madurodam started as just a model of a castle. Then it began to grow into a town around a castle—just as real towns often did. Canals and houses were added—and then department stores, parks, a railway, a seaport and then a modern airport.

At night, this model town is lit up, every street lamp and house having its lights on. Every visitor to Holland tries to see the miniature town of Madurodam.

Because Holland's coast-line is so long and sandy, it has many seaside resorts with miles and miles of beaches.

Side-by-side with The Hague is Holland's largest and most modern seaside resort—Scheveningen. This has a wide and busy sea-front and a broad, sandy beach.

Nearby is the old fishing village of the same name. From this harbour sails one of Holland's fine, modern fishing fleets.

There are several of these fishing harbours along the coast. One is shown in the picture opposite.

Halfway between Rotterdam and The Hague is the lovely old town of Delft. It is probably one of the most attractive towns in Holland. Here again are many tree-lined canals and elegant houses built in the 16th and 17th centuries.

Here lived and worked the great Dutch artist Vermeer, about whom you can read in the Ladybird series—'Great Artists'. He painted pictures of the homes and domestic life in Holland during the 17th century.

In this town is made the world-famous blue and white Delft pottery. More than three hundred artists are employed at the factory where it is made. Each piece of Delft pottery is hand-painted by these artists.

In some parts of Holland, national costume is still worn every day. There are also special costumes which are kept for certain occasions. National costumes are mostly to be seen in the country districts and on the islands along the coast. They are seldom seen in the modern, large towns.

In the past, each region of Holland had its own costume, which was worn by everyone in that region.

Two places where you will be sure to see national costume are Volendam and Marken. In Marken the little boys are dressed like girls—in bibs, bonnets and aprons.

It is sad that these charming and colourful clothes are not suitable for modern, industrial life and are being worn less and less.

Holland is a country of bicycles. You will see them everywhere, ridden by young and old people. Nuns and priests ride bicycles, and even young children are carried on them. You will see bicycles in all sorts of places—in streets, in houses, on the trains and even in cloakrooms kept only for bicycles.

Many roads have special sections for cyclists so they need not be in danger from motor cars. Many cyclists fix small petrol engines to their bicycles. They can then travel much greater distances at higher speeds.

Take especial care when crossing roads, as drivers keep to their right-hand side instead of their left as in Great Britain.

The Dutch are a nation of flower-lovers. If a house has a garden, it is usually full of flowers, however small the garden may be. If there is no garden, then there are flowers in pots and vases everywhere around the house or flat.

In the streets you can see flower-carts delivering bunches of blooms to houses. People like to give one another flowers for all sorts of reasons. If a Dutchman comes to see you at your home, he is likely to bring a bunch of flowers.

Another sight you are likely to see in a Dutch city is one of the large, decorated, mechanical organs which are dragged around the streets and played to passers-by. One is shown in the picture opposite.

The Dutch people love music and paintings. Many of the small, country towns have their own orchestras, and every village has at least a brass band.

There are many art galleries and museums in Holland. Some of the world's greatest painters lived in the Netherlands—Rembrandt, Peter de Hooch, Vermeer, Frans Hals, Peiter Bruegel and others. Some of these painters, like Vermeer, loved to paint the interiors of the Dutch homes of their time, and the sort of activities that went on inside and outside. Houses, brickwork, furniture, domestic utensils and activities were all painted with loving care and in great detail.

Art galleries in Holland are always full of admirers of these artists, even in winter when visitors have gone. In the picture opposite we see a Dutchman studying closely the details of Rembrandt's famous painting—'The Night Watch'.

Besides producing bulbs, flowers and farm produce for sale to other countries, the Dutch have large electrical industries making radios, record players, lighting fittings and many other electrical goods for export. Some of the largest of these factories are at Eindhoven in southern Holland.

Also in the south of Holland is Maastricht. Here are pottery, glass and paper-making industries.

At Rotterdam is a fine ship-building industry. Huge ocean-going liners are built there. The S.S.-Rotterdam—a famous Dutch liner which sails regularly to New York, was built there.

HOLLAND

More than half of Holland lies below sea-level
and 7% is covered by lakes, rivers and canals,
not including the Zuider Zee.
Since 1900 the area of the land has increased
by 800 square miles (2072 square kilometres)
due to the reclamation of the land from
the water.

SOME INTERESTING PLACES TO VISIT

Amsterdam - Rijksmuseum (16th-19th century
paintings). Stedelijk Museum (Modern art).
Historical Shipping Museum. Diamond cutting
establishments.

Arnhem - Open-air Museum (farms, windmills,
costumes). Safari lion park.

Delft - De Porceleyne Fles (Delft pottery;
demonstrations and showrooms).

Eindhoven - Evoluon (permanent Philips
exhibition depicting evolution of industry,
science and technology in modern society).

Groningen - Northern Shipping Museum.

Haarlem - Frans Hals Museum (portraits by
Frans Hals and paintings by Haarlem masters
from the 16th century to the present day).

The Hague - Miniature City of Madurodam.
Peace Palace (seat of the International Court
of Justice). Stamp Museum.

Heerenveen - Two-wheeler Museum.

Kaatsheuvel (north of Tilburg) - De Efteling.
Fairytale Park, especially for children.

Leek (near Groningen) - "Nienoord" National
Carriage Museum.

Leidschendam - National Automobile
Museum.

Leiden - National Museum of Ethnology.

Overloon - Netherlands National War and
Resistance Museum.

Utrecht - Gold, Silver and Clock Museum.
Music Box and Street Organ Museum.

This inset map shows th[e]
Zuider Zee before the la[nd]

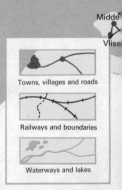

Midde[l]

Vliss[ingen]

Towns, villages and roads

Railways and boundaries

Waterways and lakes